Endorsements

"Take a trip with me on a journey through forgiveness. People young and old traumatized and often even scarred due to the happenings of life, struggle to find the strength to break away from past hurts. This book is a guide to the process of forgiveness and letting go. You will experience the pain of unforgiveness, and give way to resurrection life. My friend, Henry Butler has been graced through the pages of *BETRAYAL* to help each reader find their pathway to freedom.

Pastor Ron Carpenter
Redemption Church

"You cannot heal what you choose to hide. You cannot love what you're unwilling to forgive." Secrets like these hold deep within them the raw power and wisdom to utterly change the outcomes of your life. Until you forgive...yourself, your spouse, your upbringing, and all else that holds you to a former experience...your future will lie in jeopardy. In my estimation, Apostle Henry Butler is a premier voice in the realm of inner healing and breakthrough through the profound revelation of divine forgiveness. If you're wondering what life could look like after betrayal, rejection, and the devastation of distrust — This book is for you. The insights hidden within, if genuinely applied to your life, will free you forever.

Duaine Johnson
Founder of DJM and Dominion University, Director of Redemption Fellowship

BETRAYAL

You Cannot Love What You're Unwilling to Forgive

BETRAYAL

You Cannot Love What You're Unwilling to Forgive

HENRY T. BUTLER JR.

GOTM
FORGIVENESS FOREVER

Betrayal © 2023 by Henry T. Butler Jr. All rights reserved.

Published by GreatnessMakers.com

All rights reserved. This book contains material protected under international and federal copyright laws and treaties. Any unauthorized reprint or use of this material is prohibited. No part of this book may be reproduced or transmitted in any form or by any means, electronic or mechanical, including photocopying, recording, or by any information storage and retrieval system, without express written permission from the author.

Identifiers:
ISBN: 979-8-9879354-9-1 (paperback)
ISBN: 979-8-9899739-9-6 (hardcover)
ISBN: 979-8-9879354-8-4 (ebook)

Available in paperback, hardcover, and e-book.

Unless otherwise indicated, all Scripture quotations are from Scripture taken from the New King James Version®. Copyright © 1982 by Thomas Nelson. Used by permission. All rights reserved.

Scripture taken from *THE MESSAGE (MSG)*. Copyright © 1993, 1994, 1995, 1996, 2000, 2001, 2002. Used by permission of NavPress Publishing Group.

Scripture quotations from The Authorized (King James) Version. Rights in the Authorized Version in the United Kingdom are vested in the Crown. Reproduced by permission of the Crown's patentee, Cambridge University Press

COPYRIGHT

Scripture quotations marked (NLT) are taken from the Holy Bible, New Living Translation, copyright ©1996, 2004, 2015 by Tyndale House Foundation. Used by permission of Tyndale House Publishers, Carol Stream, Illinois 60188. All rights reserved.

Any Internet addresses (websites, blogs, etc.) and telephone numbers printed in this book are offered as a resource. They are not intended in any way to be or imply an endorsement by Greatness Makers, nor does Greatness Makers vouch for the content of these sites and numbers for the life of this book.

Contents

1. Harmless Conversations — 1
2. Regret — 5
3. Revenge — 9
4. Unforgiveness — 13
5. Let's Heal — 19
6. Overcoming — 23
7. Cycles — 25

BONUS SECTION — 27

Day One — 29

Day Two — 31

Day Three — 33

Day Four — 35

Day Five — 39

Day Six — 43

Day Seven	47
Day Eight	49
Day Nine	51
Day Ten	53
Day Eleven	55
Day Twelve	57
Day Thirteen	59
Day Fourteen	61
Day Fifteen	63
Day Sixteen	65
Day Seventeen	67
Day Eighteen	69
Day Nineteen	71
Day Twenty	75
Day Twenty-One	77
Day Twenty-Two	79
Day Twenty-Three	81
Day Twenty-Four	83
Day Twenty-Five	87
Day Twenty-Six	89

Day Twenty-Seven	91
Day Twenty-Eight	93
Day Twenty-Nine	95
Day Thirty	97
About The Author	101

Dedication

First and foremost, to my Lord and Savior JESUS CHRIST, for without Him nothing is possible, but with Him, all things are possible. To my parents who love me and my brother and my sister who always support me. To my beautiful wife, Kiva, and my two sons, Kyle and Joshua. To you, the reader, whom without your transparency to admit that the betrayal in your life has warped your decision-making and changed the dynamics of your household, I may not have written this book. It's to shed light on a generational matter and to give principles on how to overcome betrayal and not to just accept it as a way of living. I want to give a special shout out to Apostle Ron Carpenter and his wife Pastor Hope Carpenter for always encouraging us as leaders to go for it; not just by telling us to do it, but by doing it themselves as examples of what God can do through you when faith is applied to kingdom principles on a consistent basis. Also, Apostle Duaine Johnson, you took out time to walk me down the lonely road of learning all over again and May the Lord bless you and your family mightily for your extreme patience. I owe you, bro, and I intend to be a blessing to you. Pastor Colson, thank you for not giving up on me and my vision. You, too, are an example of why I can't quit. Thank you, sir!

Chapter One
Harmless Conversations

BETRAYAL (Regret, Unforgiveness, Revenge)

Ok, brace yourselves! This is not a book of rebuke or another rant about people and why life is so difficult. I believe we all suffer in one way or another from the spirit of betrayal and until we uncover its hiding place and learn how to deal with it properly, we won't be able to successfully move forward in life at all.

It is because of the spirit of betrayal that so many people have fallen away from faith in Jesus. They don't trust what they've heard about God or they just refuse to believe in themselves and they've given up on life.

With that being said, let's lay some foundation. Betrayal happened first in the heavenly realm. Lucifer betrayed his realm when he trafficked where man would rule. He tries to get us to traffic where he rules. By not understanding or knowing who you are and what the Word says concerning your life, you end up trafficking in an area where Satan rules (darkness).

Satan knows that if you don't know who you are, and if you don't know the message of the Kingdom, he can easily talk you out of what you do not know that you have. In an innocent conversation, humanity literally handed Satan our inheritance. We truly perish from the lack of knowledge. As a result, Satan is allowed to traffic in what we do not know.

The word *betrayal* in the Greek means, 'to hand over.' I've got a question for you. What have you handed over that you wish you had held on to? What have you once possessed and ignorantly gave away because you didn't understand its value? It's not too late to take back what's yours. Nevertheless, it can be challenging to get started in the right direction. Yes, challenging, but not impossible.

QUESTIONS:

1. What conversations have you had with someone that brought hurt, but you didn't realize they intended to mean you harm?

2. How can you make an effort to get over the betrayal instead of getting even?

3. Has being betrayed caused you to become a betrayer?

Chapter Two
Regret

I remember getting rid of cars, shoes, and even business relationships with people and being left with regret and later on, all I had to show for it was a memory full of what ifs!

That's number one when it comes to betrayal, the spirit of regret. Deep regret from not getting the promotion, or the house. Regret about what you said and realizing you can't take those words back. Regret from never apologizing about something that now seems so ridiculous.

Listen to this, one of man's weaknesses is that he talks too much and he responds inaccurately so Satan interrogates our decisions in hopes of us speaking without thinking.

The regret of not being able to take back what was said or done can be detrimental to every other decision that you make.

One definition of regret is: **sorrow aroused by circumstances beyond one's control or power to repair**. The inability of being able to fix a situation that is constantly causing discomfort in your life and others can create barriers that can put the brakes on future accomplishments.

In this world, we need people to help us but sometimes, because of regret, we remain in a cycle and it continues over and over. As a result, revenge is birthed.

Before we go into what I think is one of the greatest struggles we deal with (Revenge), let's ask ourselves a question. Is it regret that we have for what we did or did not do? Or is it revenge?

Sometimes we can think that we're living our best life, but in actuality, we're getting revenge on everything that we regretted that happened or didn't happen.

Let me give you a quick example of what that looks like. It's when you're moving forward in life, but constantly having to do things over and over again. It's like you're getting nowhere.

And that's because revenge is a cycle of unforgiveness and though you say you love what you're doing (love is the principle thing), you cannot love what you're unwilling to forgive.

So, in reality, you're not really moving forward, but you're getting revenge on not moving forward in your past. I like to call this rerun seasons.

Do you feel as if your life has entered a season of reruns? We can change this by dealing with the root of where all of this began. If we don't deal with it, there will be consequences. Unhealed regret leads to unhinged revenge.

Questions:

1. If you could change anything about the past; what would it be and why?

2. What do you regret that you feel like there's no restitution for?

3. Have you taken the steps to heal from it ?

Chapter Three
Revenge

A teachable spirit and a humbleness to admit your ignorance or your mistake will save you a lot of pain. However, if you're a person who knows it all, then you've got a lot of heavy-hearted experiences coming your way. — Ron Carpenter, Jr.

Revenge is like high blood pressure because it can go undetected for years. A lot of times revenge is called, 'Doing the right thing', or you know 'I just don't talk to them or deal with them anymore.'

Sometimes revenge is not you avoiding an individual, but - on the contrary - you stay in their face all the time. You know that they don't deal with you, so you come around anyway as a way of getting revenge.

Revenge is the act of revenging, retaliation for injuries or wrongs, vengeance, something done in vengeance, the desire to retaliate, vindictiveness.

The Bible records the message this way: *'Don't hit back, discover beauty in everyone. If you've got it in you, get along with everybody.'*

Don't insist on getting even; that's not for you to do. "I'll do the judging," says God. "I'll take care of it."

Our Scriptures tell us that *"if you see your enemy hungry, go buy that person lunch, or if he's thirsty, get him a drink. Your generosity will surprise him with goodness. Don't let evil get the best of you; get the best of evil by doing good."* (Romans 12:17-21 MSG)

Revenge is a lifestyle of incomplete dreams. Attempting to get revenge on others has caused some people to never become who they were created to be.

Goals are never met when you live for revenge. *'Vengeance is mine sayeth the Lord'* is what's written so when I take matters into my own hands, the ramifications from doing that only cause the spirit of revenge to grow even more. Because when getting even with flesh and blood is my goal, I'll be chasing false hope and dreams forever because God has already won for me through Jesus's death on the cross.

Colossians 2:15 says that *"the cross was a triumphant victory."*

Regret and revenge are incredible enemies, but I don't believe that they're worse than unforgiveness. But before we go there, let's observe something here when it pertains to revenge.

Is your retaliation affecting the people or persons it's aimed towards or is it only affecting you? Most of the time, retaliation and revenge only affects the person that's giving it and the people that's connected to the giver.

Sometimes, the person you've aimed your revenge towards doesn't even know that your rage or your revenge exists. Grudges are built between family members who feel betrayed and revenge becomes a lifestyle, always competing for image and likeness.

The spirit of revenge is literally the parent of our identity crisis in the world. No one knows who they are because they are always attempting to create an identity to get revenge on what they're not. Instead of seeking the Kingdom, they seek the world. Instead of transforming; they conform. The root of bitterness that all of this is connected to is Unforgiveness.

LIFE IS NOT SHORT; YOU'RE JUST WASTING TIME.

Questions:

1. Was it a person, place or thing that you want revenge on?

2. Do you remember what started it?

3. Is it your revenge or is it generational?

Chapter Four
Unforgiveness

I know that even with Scripture and the fact that we believe that what God said in his word through His grace is sufficient, the bitter root of unforgiveness can hijack every plan and thought you may have had of letting go of grudges.

Trying our best to avoid people doesn't remove the problem. Bringing it up saying that you're good, when you know you're probably not, isn't helping nor is it healthy. Unforgiveness can spread through your family like stage 4 cancer and, by the time it's detected, nobody touches it because it's too painful to talk about or they are just too tired of reliving it.

Sometimes what our parents never dealt with, but tried to beat out of us, has become the same enemy that we're wrestling with. We can hold a grudge against upbringing because of it. Some people got comfortable in not dealing with matters of the heart and the danger in that is that being comfortable cripples you so now you don't attempt to fix anything, you just settle for "I guess that's just how it goes."

We struggle with what we do not know how to deal with and it's easier to say "God's got it or God knows my heart, than to actually take the responsibility of seeking the Kingdom so that all these things can be added unto you.

The responsibility of being a child of God is hard especially when you're attempting to get revenge for being a child of your environment, color, financial situations, or any other thing that's the opposite of what God has said or of what someone told me that God said.

I know that God has given us His spirit so that we can love and forgive one another. But you cannot love what you're unwilling to forgive. I know that you hear me saying this phrase or concept a lot, but that's only because it's true.

I believe that God's forgiveness is the key to it all and if you don't receive it you'll never be able to heal from anything! So then, you'll constantly be trying to get revenge on a life or a person that you need to forgive, but without God's forgiveness, you'll say that you forgave them, but your forgiveness won't let you forget, so you'll never be able to heal from what you can't let go of.

The Bible records it like this in King James Version: *"Judge not and ye shall not be judged; condemn not and ye shall not be condemned; forgive and ye shall be forgiven; give and it shall be given unto you, good measure, pressed down and shaken together, and running over, shall men give into your bosom. For with the same measure that ye mete withal it shall be measured to you again."* (Luke 6:37-38 KJV)

Please allow me to explain; the word forgiveness means 'to release the necessary things.' Jesus is God's forgiveness. He was released by God in the beginning, and He is the order to all chaos. God said, "Let there be light." The word let means to release and the word light means order to chaos in Genesis 1:3, so God released His forgiveness to a world of chaos.

When you receive Jesus, who is God's forgiveness; your life begins to get in order because His life and death, avenges yours and when you receive God's forgiveness and you're born again, you have inherited the power and position to forgive and forget .

Without God's forgiveness, you can forgive but you can't forget. Only God's forgiveness forgives and never forgets to forgive.

I understand that some unforgiveness comes from the loss of loved ones and we feel betrayed because of loss so we hang on to memories so that we never forget the person, but when your memory is attached to anger and betrayal instead of keeping the memories alive to help you heal, keeping the memories alive only causes infection and spiritual diseases and even some physical ones as well.

We have to be slow to speak because, in one conversation, we handed over everything. In the third chapter of Genesis, the serpent was more cunning than any beast of the field and Satan used him. Satan doesn't ask questions that he doesn't have the answers to; he asks rhetorical questions or he makes rhetorical statements or suggestions because he's not looking for answers, he's looking for lack of knowledge.

He doesn't care if you know the truth as long as he can get you to debate the truth you believe. He's after ignorant children of God.

As soon as you try to explain on your own, in your own words or talk about how you feel, this is an indication that you don't know your identity in Christ and without a true understanding of what God has said in his written word about a matter, you're literally handing over your inheritance because Satan doesn't have the authority to talk to you. You are royalty and in right standing and he has fallen from grace. He's under law, the written word, but you are under grace, the spoken word through the power of the HOLY SPIRIT.

That's why Jesus in Luke the 4th chapter, doesn't tell Satan how He feels; He only tells him what is written. Psalm 103:20 says that the angels harken to the word of God. Satan is a fallen angel and he harkens to the word, which is the law against him, but it is a promise for me.

But once again, when you're suffering with regret, revenge, or unforgiveness, we make our feelings our reality and your feelings are real, but they are not your reality.

So, the question is what did God do to fix the spirit of betrayal?

Questions:

1. Are you willing to go through the process of healing?

2. Is what happened worth the bitterness?

3. What have you missed because of unforgiveness?

Chapter Five
Let's Heal

*F**orgiveness is about empowering yourself, rather than empowering your past. — T.D. Jakes*

There is hope to heal from the spirit of regret, revenge, and unforgiveness, which were all birthed from the spirit of betrayal and it is God's forgiveness.

Most of the time, people don't think anything is wrong or pride has become the leader of everything that they do, so they hide what needs to be exposed. And the danger in that is that GOD CAN'T HEAL WHAT YOU HIDE.

When it comes to God's forgiveness;, we don't understand that Jesus is God's forgiveness. There is no forgiveness of sin without the shedding of the blood and who shed the blood, Jesus.

So then Jesus is God's forgiveness. God could not accept man's forgiveness because it only reminds God of what happened in the beginning (betrayal), and it won't allow Him to forget.

So He sent His forgiveness into time to not only forgive us but to heal us as well. His forgiveness healed our relationship and gave us our true identity back through Christ. His forgiveness, which is Jesus, had to come back to Him so that we could be forgiven because God's forgiveness is the only forgiveness that allows the sins, the lawlessness, and the transgressions to be remembered no more – Hebrews 10:17

God's forgiveness never forgets to forgive. God's forgiveness works in and on past, future, and present situations. God's forgiveness heals, delivers, and sets free any individual from the bondage of betrayal.

If you're struggling today with revenge, regret, or unforgiveness, this is your day to renounce those things, receive God's forgiveness, and then announce your healing, your deliverance, and your freedom which is a type of birthing because you have finally been delivered from the womb of betrayal.

He called you out of darkness into His marvelous light. Darkness is not the absence of light but it is not knowing, which is ignorance. Light is knowledge and not only knowledge, but light is also God's forgiveness. Jesus is the light of the world.

I told you all that God released His order to chaos when He said, 'Let there be light.' God released His forgiveness in the beginning so that we would be forgiven before we even began. Amazing, Hallelujah, Glory to God! I had to take a minute to praise Him because this is such Good News. Your enemy never had a chance.

Today is the day that the spirit of betrayal loosens its grip and is cast back into outer darkness. Say this with me: today I receive God's forgiveness. God's forgiveness releases what is necessary for me to be able to forgive and forget. His forgiveness allows me to let grudges go so that I can heal. And whenever something comes at me again, His forgiveness never forgets to forgive. His forgiveness which is His Word.

JESUS did not come back to Him void, but His forgiveness was accomplished in the place that God sent Him and the same forgiveness is accomplishing a work in me and my family.

Today I am forgiven and I'm full of His Spirit and I'm not under the curse of the law, but I'm under God's grace and I've been redeemed and restored to my rightful position in Christ. I'm delivered today and forever more from the spirit of regret, the spirit of revenge, and the spirit of unforgiveness.

I renounce those strongholds and imaginations, and I am announcing that my mind has been made new through the blood of Jesus Christ. I have dominion, I'm crowned with God's glory, and He's put all things under my feet, in Jesus's name, Amen, Amen, and Amen. Continue to declare this revelation and truth in your life and to your family. This is your inheritance!

Chapter Six
Overcoming

1. Admitting that you're not well is the key to exposing secrets that need to be revealed. God can't heal what you hide.

2. The source is usually from upbringing, the neglect of it or the overkill. Sometimes, because of what parents have dealt with or haven't resolved within their own lives, they take it out on their kids so when they raise their own; the process is repeated with no end in sight.

3. You need to speak to them (parents) through God's forgiveness and if they are deceased, write them a letter. The release of God's forgiveness will cause both parties to begin to heal.

4. Take small steps in building a new relationship and don't try to rebuild with old things. Use new strategies from your new way of thinking to do new things for you and your family.

Chapter Seven
Cycles

Sometimes the old things will try to resurface and try to talk you out of your new way of thinking. It's nothing more than history desiring to repeat itself, but don't forget that you've been forgiven and you walk in the identity of Christ.

Those old conversations have nothing to say to the New You! Make no doubt about it, you will be tested, but there are Alarms that will signal you when the enemy of your past is attempting to bargain with your present concerning your future.

There are always cycles of some sort in every family that try to keep a process of destruction in place, but when you can recognize the Alarms that signal their arrival you can defuse a situation that never was one to begin with. To find out more, prepare yourself for our next book.

BONUS SECTION
30 Day Devotional

Day Three

"Father, I desire that they also whom You gave Me may be with Me where I am, that they may behold My glory which You have given Me; for You loved Me before the foundation of the world."—John 17:24

"All who dwell on the earth will worship him, whose names have not been written in the Book of Life of the Lamb slain from the foundation of the world.—Revelation 13:8

This shows that God forgave us before we even began. Satan never had a chance. You're more than a conqueror because you won before your life in time began.

JOURNAL NOTES

Day One

"In fact, according to the law of Moses, nearly everything was purified with blood. For without the shedding of blood, there is no forgiveness."—Hebrews 9:22 NLT

So since Jesus shed the blood then He is God's forgiveness. God sent His forgiveness because He couldn't accept man's forgiveness. Man's forgiveness doesn't have the power to heal(to let it go, to forget).

"For I will be merciful to their unrighteousness, and their sins and their lawless deeds I will remember no more."
—Hebrews 8:12

God's forgiveness always heals and never forgets to forgive.

JOURNAL NOTES

Day Four

"Blessed be the God and Father of our Lord Jesus Christ, who has blessed us with every spiritual blessing in the heavenly places in Christ, just as He chose us in Him before the foundation of the world, that we should be holy and without blame before Him in love,"—Ephesians 1:3-4

You see; everything was already done in Christ before God said 'let there be light'. He took care of your enemy in Heaven and He took care of your enemy on Earth.

"He who sins is of the devil, for the devil has sinned from the beginning. For this purpose the Son of God was manifested, that He might destroy the works of the devil."—I John 3:8

"having wiped out the handwriting of requirements that was against us, which was contrary to us. And He has taken it out of the way, having nailed it to the cross. Having disarmed principalities and powers, He made a public spectacle of them, triumphing over them in it."—Colossians 2:14-15

Now the word of God defends your life not condemns your life.

"There is therefore now no condemnation to those who are in Christ Jesus, who do not walk according to the flesh, but according to the Spirit."—Romans 8:1

JOURNAL NOTES

Day Five

"Your eyes saw my substance, being yet unformed. And in Your book they all were written, The days fashioned for me, When as yet there were none of them."—Psalms 139:16

"Now faith is the substance of things hoped for, the evidence of things not seen. By faith we understand that the worlds were framed by the word of God, so that the things which are seen were not made of things which are visible."—Hebrews 11:1,3

"For we walk by faith, not by sight."—II Corinthians 5:7

"So then faith comes by hearing, and hearing by the word of God."—Romans 10:17

Our whole life is in our faith. When life happens to us there's a word of faith that has been prepared for us. We choose – in hope – to speak the word of God to our situation and when we do; the evidence will show up if we don't give up.

"So let's not get tired of doing what is good. At just the right time we will reap a harvest of blessing if we don't give up."—Galatians 6:9 NLT

JOURNAL NOTES

Day Six

"He gives power to the weak, And to those who have no might He increases strength. But those who wait on the Lord Shall renew their strength; They shall mount up with wings like eagles, They shall run and not be weary, They shall walk and not faint." —Isaiah 40:29, 31

"Then he said to me, "Do not fear, Daniel, for from the first day that you set your heart to understand, and to humble yourself before your God, your words were heard; and I have come because of your words. But the prince of the kingdom of Persia withstood me twenty-one days; and behold, Michael, one of the chief princes, came to help me, for I had been left alone there with the kings of Persia. Now I have come to make you understand what will happen to your people in the latter days, for the vision refers to many days yet to come." When he had spoken such words to me, I turned my face toward the ground and became speechless. And suddenly, one having the likeness

of the sons of men touched my lips; then I opened my mouth and spoke, saying to him who stood before me, "My Lord, because of the vision my sorrows have overwhelmed me, and I have retained no strength. For how can this servant of my Lord talk with you, my Lord? As for me, no strength remains in me now, nor is any breath left in me." Then again, the one having the likeness of a man touched me and strengthened me. And he said, "O man greatly beloved, fear not! Peace be to you; be strong, yes, be strong!" So when he spoke to me I was strengthened, and said, "Let my Lord speak, for you have strengthened me.""—Daniel 10:12-19

Sometimes it may seem as if God has failed you, and we can get weak in our waiting, but don't give up. Daniel waited and received His word from God. And this word strengthened him to continue his assignment.

JOURNAL NOTES

Day Seven

"And the Lord said, "That's right, and it means that I am watching, and I will certainly carry out all my plans."
—Jeremiah 1:12 NLT

"For as the rain comes down, and the snow from heaven, And do not return there, But water the earth, And make it bring forth and bud, That it may give seed to the sower And bread to the eater, So shall My word be that goes forth from My mouth; It shall not return to Me void, But it shall accomplish what I please, And it shall prosper in the thing for which I sent it."—Isaiah 55:10-11

We can be confident in knowing that when God spoke in the beginning; He continues to watch over every word and He makes sure that His word accomplishes the assignment in our lives. But we must speak the word so that He can perform that word. Faith, which is our life, will manifest in time.

JOURNAL NOTES

Day Eight

"Remember the former things of old, For I am God, and there is no other; I am God, and there is none like Me, Declaring the end from the beginning, And from ancient times things that are not yet done, Saying, 'My counsel shall stand, And I will do all My pleasure,'"—Isaiah 46:9-10

> Your life is slowly becoming who you already are.
>
> Ron Carpenter

God established our ending first so that while we live; our lives will have to make the adjustments to line up with His expected end.

JOURNAL NOTES

Day Nine

"And we know that all things work together for good to those who love God, to those who are the called according to His purpose. For whom He foreknew, He also predestined to be conformed to the image of His Son, that He might be the firstborn among many brethren. Moreover whom He predestined, these He also called; whom He called, these He also justified; and whom He justified, these He also glorified. What then shall we say to these things? If God is for us, who can be against us?"—Romans 8:28-31

This is a favorite scripture of almost everyone that I know. I love it because it shows the forgiveness of God above and beyond how we will be or what we will do before we even begin. He predestined us. *Predestined* in Greek means to mark out beforehand. I'm telling you; God didn't miss. He has thoroughly taken care of us.

JOURNAL NOTES

Day Ten

"Therefore humble yourselves under the mighty hand of God, that He may exalt you in due time, casting all your care upon Him, for He cares for you."—1 Peter 5:6-7

And God did this before the foundations of the world. We speak it so that what He has already done can manifest in time.

I included these Scriptures so that you can get an understanding of what God has done for you through Christ Jesus and how he has forgiven you. Now let's go a little deeper because we're going to make sure that you never allow the spirit of betrayal to overtake you again.

JOURNAL NOTES

GATHERINGOFTHEMULTITUDE.COM

Day Eleven

"Bless the Lord, you His angels, Who excel in strength, who do His word, Heeding the voice of His word."—Psalms 103:20

"What is man that You are mindful of him, And the son of man that You visit him? For You have made him a little lower than the angels, And You have crowned him with glory and honor. You have made him to have dominion over the works of Your hands; You have put all things under his feet,"—Psalms 8:4-6

Simply put; you are God's ambassador in the Earth and when you speak His word mixed with Faith; God backs you up. All of Eternity is backing you up. Now that's wealth!

JOURNAL NOTES

Day Twelve

"Now then, we are ambassadors for Christ, as though God were pleading through us: we implore you on Christ's behalf, be reconciled to God. For He made Him who knew no sin to be sin for us, that we might become the righteousness of God in Him." — II Corinthians 5:20-21

Jesus just didn't die for us, He died *as* us. We are confidently representing our Father and He has no resentment concerning us. Reconciliation- the process of ransoming man from his state of sin and spiritual darkness and of restoring him to a state of harmony and unity with Deity. We are forgiven!

JOURNAL NOTES

Day Thirteen

"And you, who once were alienated and enemies in your mind by wicked works, yet now He has reconciled in the body of His flesh through death, to present you holy, and blameless, and above reproach in His sight— if indeed you continue in the faith, grounded and steadfast, and are not moved away from the hope of the gospel which you heard, which was preached to every creature under heaven, of which I, Paul, became a minister."—Colossians 1:21-23

Don't let satan talk you out of your new relationship with God. God sees you as His son, not a sinner.

JOURNAL NOTES

Day Fourteen

"But as it is written: "Eye has not seen, nor ear heard, Nor have entered into the heart of man The things which God has prepared for those who love Him." But God has revealed them to us through His Spirit. For the Spirit searches all things, yes, the deep things of God." —I Corinthians 2:9-10

"But you have an anointing from the Holy One, and you know all things. I have not written to you because you do not know the truth, but because you know it, and that no lie is of the truth." —I John 2:20-21

God has hidden His truth in you and His Spirit knows all things. Knowing the word of God allows God's Spirit to lead us and guide us in life's good and tough times.

JOURNAL NOTES

Day Fifteen

"Now this is the confidence that we have in Him, that if we ask anything according to His will, He hears us. And if we know that He hears us, whatever we ask, we know that we have the petitions that we have asked of Him."—I John 5:14-15

God wants us to speak His word back to Him. It's a parent-to-child dialogue and God will not lie nor will He change His mind.

JOURNAL NOTES

Day Sixteen

"God is not a man, that He should lie, Nor a son of man, that He should repent. Has He said, and will He not do? Or has He spoken, and will He not make it good?"—Numbers 23:19

We must get to a place where the word of God is our only lifeline.

JOURNAL NOTES

Day Seventeen

"Then they cried out to the Lord in their trouble, And He saved them out of their distresses. He sent His word and healed them, And delivered them from their destructions." —Psalms 107:19-20

God is available to answer us through His word at all times because there's nothing that He hasn't already done or accomplished.

JOURNAL NOTES

Day Eighteen

"That which is has already been, And what is to be has already been; And God requires an account of what is past."—Ecclesiastes 3:15

God's word and His will is finalized in Heaven and when we speak His word; we can experience the results of His word on Earth.

JOURNAL NOTES

Day Nineteen

"My people are destroyed for lack of knowledge: because thou hast rejected knowledge, I will also reject thee, that thou shalt be no priest to me: seeing thou hast forgotten the law of thy God, I will also forget thy children."—Hosea 4:6 KJV

"The Lord is not slack concerning his promise, as some men count slackness; but is longsuffering to us-ward, not willing that any should perish, but that all should come to repentance."—2 Peter 3:9 KJV

"But ye are a chosen generation, a royal priesthood, an holy nation, a peculiar people; that ye should shew forth the praises of him who hath called you out of darkness into his marvellous light: which in time past were not a people, but are now the people of God: which had not obtained mercy, but now have obtained mercy."—1 Peter 2:9-10 KJV

Not knowing who you are and what God has done through Christ can be deadly. God's love for us is unconditional. He was so invested in this love for us that He sacrificed everything – even His only begotten Son. God trusts us. That's powerful.

JOURNAL NOTES

Day Twenty

"Then the serpent said to the woman, "You will not surely die. For God knows that in the day you eat of it your eyes will be opened, and you will be like God, knowing good and evil." So when the woman saw that the tree was good for food, that it was pleasant to the eyes, and a tree desirable to make one wise, she took of its fruit and ate. She also gave to her husband with her, and he ate."—Genesis 3:4-6

God, in Genesis 2:9, did make the tree good for food and pleasant to the eyes, but it is not written that He made it to make one wise. Satan is always trying to get us to see something that God didn't say.

JOURNAL NOTES

Day Twenty-One

"Death and life are in the power of the tongue, And those who love it will eat its fruit."—Proverbs 18:21

"So then, my beloved brethren, let every man be swift to hear, slow to speak, slow to wrath; for the wrath of man does not produce the righteousness of God."—James 1:19-20

Sometimes in our waiting; we become frustrated and we say how we feel. Feelings are real, but they're not your Godly, Eternal Reality. We walk by faith and not by sight, but when you say what you see versus what God said that you've heard; you start looking like what you're looking at. If you're focused on feeling bitter; you look bitter. When you are driven by revenge, and grudges are the road you ride on; you look like where you're headed.

JOURNAL NOTES

Day Twenty-Two

"My brethren, count it all joy when you fall into various trials, knowing that the testing of your faith produces patience. But let patience have its perfect work, that you may be perfect and complete, lacking nothing."
—James 1:2-4

The definition of patience means to be able to tolerate delay. We must build up a tolerance of knowing that it's not us that's being tested, but it is our Faith that is on trial. Faith answers the word of God not our complaints or excuses or our ignorance. The word of God will be the evidence your Faith needs when it's on trial. Remember, your faith is the life you hope for and the evidence you haven't seen yet.

JOURNAL NOTES

Day Twenty-Three

"If we say that we have no sin, we deceive ourselves, and the truth is not in us. If we confess our sins, He is faithful and just to forgive us our sins and to cleanse us from all unrighteousness."—I John 1:8-9

Own it! Whatever it is that you think is so bad that God won't forgive you is just one of your enemy's schemes. Satan is lying to you. Don't hide things that God has forgiven you of. God can't heal what you hide.

JOURNAL NOTES

GATHERINGOFTHEMULTITUDE.COM

Day Twenty-Four

"Judge not, and ye shall not be judged: condemn not, and ye shall not be condemned: forgive, and ye shall be forgiven: give, and it shall be given unto you; good measure, pressed down, and shaken together, and running over, shall men give into your bosom. For with the same measure that ye mete withal it shall be measured to you again."—Luke 6:37-38 KJV

When we hold grudges against others, that is very dangerous. It blocks blessings. What if you're holding a grudge against someone that of whom God has chosen to bless you. A lot of people are betrayed because of racism and prejudice and without God's forgiveness, you will not be able to recover from that betrayal. A lot of people are poor right now or not doing as great as they could because they are holding onto a grudge against the person(s) that God is waiting to use.

Receive God's forgiveness today so that the wealth of Heaven can overtake you. It's not just money; it's also peace.

JOURNAL NOTES

GATHERINGOFTHEMULTITUDE.COM

Day Twenty-Five

"Brethren, I count not myself to have apprehended: but this one thing I do, forgetting those things which are behind, and reaching forth unto those things which are before, I press toward the mark for the prize of the high calling of God in Christ Jesus."—Philippians 3:13-14 KJV

Stay focused!

Jesus became your story and made your story, His-story, *history*! Did you catch that? There is a future ahead of you it's got your name on it. Stop letting the past be the company you keep.

JOURNAL NOTES

GATHERINGOFTHEMULTITUDE.COM

Day Twenty-Six

"But God, who is rich in mercy, because of His great love with which He loved us, even when we were dead in trespasses, made us alive together with Christ (by grace you have been saved), and raised us up together, and made us sit together in the heavenly places in Christ Jesus,"—Ephesians 2:4-6

God didn't wait on you. You are already saved!

JOURNAL NOTES

Day Twenty-Seven

"For by grace you have been saved through faith, and that not of yourselves; it is the gift of God, not of works, lest anyone should boast. For we are His workmanship, created in Christ Jesus for good works, which God prepared beforehand that we should walk in them."— Ephesians 2:8-10

As we have previously discussed; God, before time began; has done a work in you. You can't work for it; you can only receive it so that it can work for you.

JOURNAL NOTES

Day Twenty-Eight

"For the weapons of our warfare are not carnal but mighty in God for pulling down strongholds, casting down arguments and every high thing that exalts itself against the knowledge of God, bringing every thought into captivity to the obedience of Christ,"—II Corinthians 10:4-5

"For indeed the gospel was preached to us as well as to them; but the word which they heard did not profit them, not being mixed with faith in those who heard it."—Hebrews 4:2

We must be confident and have faith in God's word when we speak.

JOURNAL NOTES

Day Twenty-Nine

"But without faith it is impossible to please Him, for he who comes to God must believe that He is, and that He is a rewarder of those who diligently seek Him."—Hebrews 11:6

Most people seek awards from people instead of a reward from God. An award could bless you, but a reward could bless a nation.

JOURNAL NOTES

Day Thirty

"But seek first the kingdom of God and His righteousness, and all these things shall be added to you."—Matthew 6:33

Be determined to do it God's way. His will outweighs our wants and our won'ts.

"And He said to me, "My grace is sufficient for you, for My strength is made perfect in weakness." Therefore most gladly I will rather boast in my infirmities, that the power of Christ may rest upon me. Therefore I take pleasure in infirmities, in reproaches, in needs, in persecutions, in distresses, for Christ's sake. For when I am weak, then I am strong."—II Corinthians 12:9-10

The very thing we could be asking God to remove may be the very reason that we walk in great power. There is nothing that God hasn't done to make sure that we are well-equipped to win.

JOURNAL NOTES

About The Author

Henry Thomas Butler Jr was born in a small town in Elberton, Georgia, called Dewy Rose. He owned a barbershop, a lawn care service, and a salon. Upon getting married to his wife, Kiva K Butler, he moved to Greenville, South Carolina, with their two children; Kyle and Joshua. He let go of those businesses to pursue the Life God chose for him; preaching the message of the Kingdom.

He's not just an author; he is also a John Maxwell Leadership coach, counselor, consultant ,and mentor. He is also a care pastor at Redemption East where his pastors are Ron and Hope Carpenter.

His ministry, Gathering of the Multitude, is also a part of Redemption Fellowship; which is the ministry network of Redemption that is set under the leadership of Apostle Duaine Johnson.

He also has a brand, Wipe Your Eyes Change Your Grip, which is also a television show that he is currently developing. He travels and does outreach; and enjoys exercising, cooking, and reading. His passion is to introduce the world to their true identity and through the power of God's forgiveness, help rebuild families and bring them back together again with the mindset of the Kingdom.

Connect with Henry at **gatheringofthemultitude.com**

ABOUT THE AUTHOR

COMING SOON!

ALARMS!
The Three Levels of Awakening

Henry Butler's Next Book
Available 2024

www.ingramcontent.com/pod-product-compliance
Lightning Source LLC
Chambersburg PA
CBHW050322010526
44119CB00003B/69